WESTMINSTER ABBEY

TEXT: TREVOR BEESON
Canon of Westminster

22th Edition

I.S.B.N. 84-378-0854-5

Dep. Legal B. 1351-2003

DISTRIBUTOR: FISA (GREAT BRITAIN) Ltd. - 22 B, Wolsey Road
LONDON N. 1 - Telephone: 020 7254 0976

Editorial Escudo de Oro, S.A.

Ten statues of 20th century christian martyrs on the west front.

The West Towers ▷

A ROYAL AND SAINTLY FOUNDER

Westminster Abbey — more correctly, the Collegiate Church of St. Peter in Westminster — is the most famous church in the English-speaking world and one of the world's great religious temples. Its stones and monuments tell a story of English history over more than nine centuries. It houses the shrine of the only English king to be recognised as a saint. Since 1066 it has been a Coronation church. During the Middle Ages it was the monastery of a community of Benedictine monks. For more than a thousand years worship and prayer have been offered on its site. Small wonder that it attracts visitors from every part of the globe and is generally crowded with pilgrims and tourists.

The origins of Westminster Abbey are lost in the mists of history. There is an ancient tradition that the founder was Sebert, King of the East Saxons in the early years of the seventh century, and this same tradition asserts that when Mellitus, the first Bishop of London, came to consecrate the new church he was informed by a Thames fisherman that this task had already been carried out by St. Peter, the Prince of the Apostles. There is no historical foundation for any of this, though King Sebert and Bishop Mellitus certainly existed and up to the fourteenth century a fisherman presented the Westminster monks with a tithe of the salmon caught in the river on St. Peter's Day — allegedly in obedience to an instruction given by St. Peter at the time of the consecration.

Two other signposts offer more realiable guidance to the past. An early charter records the granting of a piece of land to a religious community in Wesminster by King Offa of Mercia in 785. This charter may not be genuine but it is certainly very old and even if spurious is likely to express an accepted tradition.

King Edgar (957-75) also granted land to a community of Benedictine monks that had been installed at Westminster by St. Dunstan about 960. His charter refers to a church with ruined chapels, which was probably a small Saxon building on the Isle of Thorns

— a remote area of land surrounded by marshes and creeks near the River Thames. Nothing remains of this church, the land has been drained and Westminster is now a seat of government as well as the site of a magnificent abbey.

History becomes much clearer from the eleventh century onwards. Edward, the last but one of England's Saxon Kings, spent his early years in France where, as a young prince, he had been driven by Danish invaders. He was a somewhat volatile character, liable to extremes of mirth and anger, and with an obsession for hunting. Under the influence of Norman monks, however, he developed a deep piety and made a vow that if ever he reached the English throne he would make a pilgrimage of gratitude to Rome — to the grave of St. Peter. In 1042 Edward returned to England as king and had every intention of fulfilling his vow, but his advisers counselled against his leaving the country again, so he sent representatives to Rome to seek a dispensation. The Pope granted this on condition that Edward should build or restore a monastery dedicated to St. Peter.

Pilgrims at the mediaeval shrine (top)

The shrine today (bottom)

The Saxon community at Wesminster was chosen for this purpose. It was described at the time as a small monastery, housing only twelve monks, with insignificant buildings and endowments so slender that they provided the monks with no more than their daily bread. Under the King's patronage, and with a new abbot, Edwin, in charge, a large monastery in the French Romanesque, or Norman, style was erected, as a replacement. This was to be the precursor of many great Norman buildings in England and took about 15 years to complete.

Edward established his own royal palace alongside the new monastery and was looking forward to the completion and dedication of his project when, towards the end of 1065, he became seriously ill. The dedication ceremony was advanced to Holy Innocents' Day (28 December) of that year, but Edward was too ill to attend and his place was taken by Queen Edith. According to one tradition, the strains of music from the church reached the King's room and he was heard to murmur, "The work stands finished". He died a few days later.

Edward's body was buried in front of the high altar of the new church on 6 January 1066 and soon his grave was visited by crowds of pilgrims who had heard stories of his personal holiness. In 1161 he was canonised as St. Edward the Confessor and two years later his body was transferred to a splendid shrine built in the Abbey by King Henry II. The cult of St. Edward had by this time become so popular that the Abbey's founder was in effect England's national saint.

Nothing remains of King Edward's church above ground. A panel of the Bayeux Tapestry (1070) gives a striking indication of its great size, shewing that the building was of cruciform shape, with a central tower capped by a small dome. Some Norman-French verse dating from the thirteenth century refers to the Abbey's two western towers, which were presumably built after the Confessor's death, and also to a lead roof. This verse goes on to mention the monastic buildings around the church —cloister, chapter house, refectory and dormitory— but does not describe them.

The Dark Cloister

Excavations carried out in the present century have located large portions of the foundations of the Norman church. These show that it was indeed a very large building —just a little shorter in length than the present Abbey— and in the England of the eleventh century it must have presented a remarkable sight, in terms both of its bulk and of its architectural splendour. The barrel-vaulted passage way (the Dark Cloister) which now leads from the Great Cloister, and the Undercroft nearby, is all that is to be seen today of King Edward's great vision and achievement.

But the memory of Edward himself is very much alive. His bones still lie in the much battered shrine behind the High Altar which is visited by thousands of people every day. On 13 October every year, special services are held to commemorate the movement of his body to a shrine in 1163, and on 28 December the celebrations of Christmas reach their climax with a Dedication Festival service. On that day a congregation which fills the Abbey to overflowing sings Christmas carols and also gives thanks for a saintly king whose political achievements were modest but who, in the foundation of Wesminster Abbey, made an indelible mark on English history.

Flying buttresses seen from the Great Cloister

A ROYAL ARTIST

Soon after Edward the Confessor's death, and following the brief reign of Harold II, England was occupied by the Normans and on Christmas Day 1066 William the Conqueror was crowned king in Westminster Abbey. The choice of this church for the Coronation was influenced by his hope that the English people would regard him as Edward's legitimate successor. Since then every English Sovereign, apart from Edward V in the fifteenth century and Edward VIII in the twentieth century, has been crowned in the Abbey. Of these kings and queens, Westminster Abbey owes most to Henry III for its present glorious architecture. Born in 1207, Henry was the first really English king for several generations. He broke with tradition by be-

ing crowned in Gloucester, because he had enemies in and around Westminster, but his ministers apologised to the Abbot and later Henry was crowned again in the Abbey — the first and only monarch to be crowned twice.

Like Edward the Confessor, whom he greatly admired, Henry was a man of deep personal piety. He was also a considerable artist and, as a result of his travels in Europe, conceived the idea of replacing the solid, fortress-like, Norman abbey at Westminster with a more graceful building in the new Gothic style then being developed in France. In 1245 the demolition of King Edward's Abbey began and before long the building now recognisable all over the world as Westminster Abbey was taking shape.

The stone came mainly from Reigate, in Surrey, while the hard marble-like stone for the main pillars was quarried at Purbeck, in Dorset, and the more malleable stone for the windows and mouldings was brought from Caen, in Normandy. At certain periods as many as 800 craftsmen and labourers were working on the new Abbey, under the direction of Master Mason Henry de Reyns, and for almost a century the site was a scene of great activity. The cost of the work was met by the king, whose enthusiasm was somewhat greater than his resources: he was driven to sell gold plate to meet the bills, and in 1267 had to retrieve and pawn the precious jewels which he had previously given for the adornment of the Confessor's shrine.

By the middle of 1269 the money had run out, the new choir of the church was completed, together with the four chapels of the apse, the transepts, and the bays which constitute the present choir and the east end of the nave. On 13 October of that year, being an important feast day of St. Edward, the work was dedicated and opened. At this point the building as a whole must have had a strange appearance, for the greater part of the nave was still in the old Norman style, with a much lower roof.

College Garden — originally the monastery garden and reputed to be the oldest garden in England

More than a century was to pass before building operations could be resumed. Simon de Langham, who had become Abbot in 1348 and was subsequently appointed Archbishop of Canterbury and a Cardinal, bequeathed a substantial sum of money to his community and this was used by another distinguished Abbot, Nicholas de Litlyngton, to start the rebuilding of the nave.

The work was continued under the enthusiastic patronage of King Richard II and good progress was made until the end of the fourteenth century. Richard's successor, Henry IV, showed little interest in the project, however, and it was left to the great King Henry V to provide 1,000 marks a year to enable the work to go on. In 1415 it was possible to use the partially completed nave for a thanksgiving service for victory at the Battle of Agincourt, but the west end of the church was not reached until 1506. The two western towers were added in the 18th century and were largely the work of Nicholas Hawksmoor, a pupil and friend of Sir Christopher Wren who had himself been architect to the Abbey during the early years of that century.

Although the rebuilding of the nave extended over 150 years, the master masons in charge of the work kept closely to Henry de Reyns's original design, so that today the entire building, apart from the Chapel of King Henry VII, appears to have been erected in one continuous operation. More than any other church in England, Westminster Abbey expresses the spirit and style of French Gothic architecture, and the influence of the cathedrals at Amiens and Rheims (it-

self a Coronation church) and Sainte-Chapelle, in Paris, is quite clear.

This influence is most marked in the contrast between the great height (103 feet) of the roof and the comparatively narrow width (35 feet) of the nave — a proportion of almost three to one which gives a most dramatic and inspiring effect. Other French features include the rounded apse at the east end, the chapels radiating from the apse, and the large rose windows in the transepts. Externally, the long series of flying buttresses, designed to take the thrust of the roof and support walls with large windows, also speak of France, rather than of England.

Yet Westminster Abbey is not simply a great French church on the banks of the Thames. There are distinctive English features to support the view that Henry de Reyns was not a French master mason, as is sometimes supposed, but an Englishman steeped in the European culture of his time which knew no national frontiers. The beautiful triforium gallery of the Abbey and the roof vaulting are more English than French; so also is the elaborate carving and sculpture of the interior stonework in the eastern half of the building.

What is no longer visible to the twentieth century eye, except in a few tantalising fragments, is the riot of colour that met the pilgrim and worshipper who entered the Abbey in the Middle Ages; the walls were covered with paintings of saints and kings. Other parts of the building, including the roof vaulting and the tombs, were ablaze with red and blue and gold. The windows gleamed like jewels, and the shrine of the Confessor was adorned with precious artefacts appropriate to a royal saint. The Abbey offered, in high art, a pre-view of heaven, and even today its soaring arches and perfect proportions help to make infinity visible.

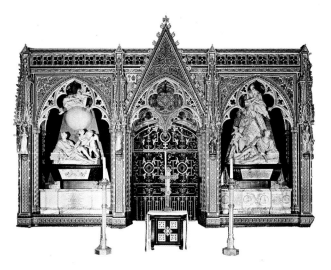

13th century wall painting of The Incredulity of St. Thomas (top left)

13th century sedilia and paintings of kings (top right)

Carved angel on the 13th century tomb of Queen Eleanor of Castile (bottom left)

The South Transept (bottom right)

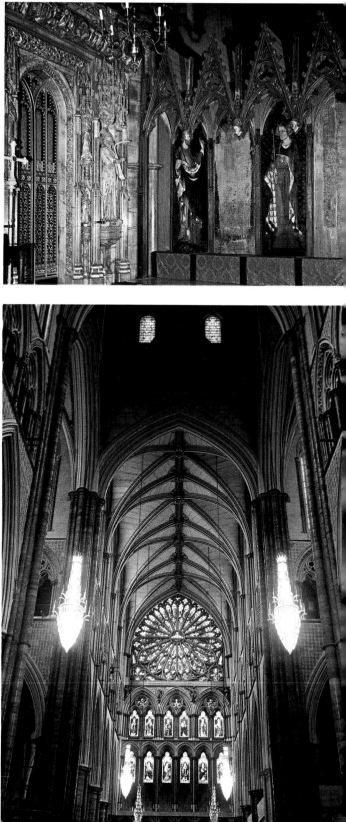

The North Aisle of the Choir and the Nave

The High Altar (top)

The Choir, looking West (bottom)

IN HEAVENLY HARMONY

Westminster Abbey was built primarily for worship. The community of Benedictine monks who lived in the Abbey for the first 500 years of its existence gathered every day to offer Mass at the altar. They also met seven times a day in the choir of their great church to recite the Divine Office, which consisted of Psalms, Bible readings and prayers. The wanton destruction in 1775 of the choir stalls dating from the time of King Henry III was perhaps the most senseless act of vandalism ever perpetrated on the Abbey. The present stalls were placed in the choir in 1848.

Today the sanctuary and choir of Westminster Abbey are best known as the backcloth of Coronations, Royal Weddings and other great state occasions when distinctive ceremonial and fine music combine to produce memorable acts of worship. But daily worship of a less elaborate kind is the mainstay of the Abbey's life. The Holy Communion (known sometimes as the Eucharist or the Mass) is celebrated in one or other of the Abbey's chapels twice every day, and at the High Altar on Sundays and other festivals of the church's year. Matins is sung on Sundays and said daily, while Evensong is sung every day except Wednesday. During the course of a year as many as 50 special services are held for national and international organisations and events, and a brief period of prayer is observed every hour when the building is open to visitors.

The priests who comprise the Dean and Chapter are involved in leading the worship, but the Choral Foundation, which includes the Precentor, the Organist and Master of the Choristers, 12 Lay Vicars and 22 Choristers and Singing Boys have the most prominent role in the choral services. The Lay Vicars are professional musicians who devote part of their musical careers to Westminster Abbey, while the Choristers, whose ages range from 8-13, reside and are educated at the Abbey Choir School in Dean's Yard.

The marriage of Princess Anne and Captain Mark Phillips

*The Funeral
of Earl
Mountbatten*

Tomb of King Henry III (top)

Memorial to Henry Purcell (bottom)

The official history of the Choral Foundation goes back to the time of Queen Elizabeth I, but there were 12 laymen singers and 10 choristers during the reign of King Henry VIII, and even earlier, in 1479, there was a Song School. During the seventeenth and eighteenth centuries, when the office of Organist was generally combined with responsibility for music at the Chapel Royal, the post was often held by one of the most distinguished musicians in the nation.

Among these musicians was Orlando Gibbons, described in his own day as "the English Palestrina", who became Organist in 1623. Many of his compositions are still in use, in all parts of the world. John Blow, who was appointed in 1669, was another musician of European repute but he resigned in 1679 to make way for his pupil, Henry Purcell.

Purcell, whose father had been a Lay Vicar, was only 21 when he became Organist but he had by this time already composed many anthems. He was undoubtedly a genius and is regarded as the greatest of English musicians, dividing his time between the Abbey, the Chapel Royal, the Court and the London theatre. On his death, at the early age of 37, John Blow returned and remained Organist for a further 13 years.

In the twentieth century the development of mass communications has placed the choir of Westminster Abbey on an international stage where, day by day, it contributes to the worship music of the very highest order.

Exterior of King Henry VII's Chapel

Fan-vaulted ceiling of the Chapel

A MOST HONOURABLE CHAPEL

The eastern-most chapel of Westminster Abbey, which has the size and proportions of a large church, is one of the most beautiful buildings in the world. Generally known as the Chapel of King Henry VII, it is in fact the Lady Chapel of the Abbey and replaced an earlier chapel dedicated in honour of the Blessed Virgin Mary in 1220.

The original idea of Henry VII (1465-1509) was to provide a fitting burial place for his uncle, King Henry VI (1421-71), who it was hoped would be canonised as a saint. But the canonisation never took place, and Henry's body remained at Windsor. Henry VII then decided that, as the Chapel of St. Edward was now full of tombs, the new Lady Chapel would make a suitable resting place for himself and his family. The entire cost, about £14,000, was met by the king, who also endowed a small college of priests to say Masses in the chapel for the repose of his soul, and established a number of charities for the benefit of the poor and aged.

The foundation stone of the new chapel was laid on the king's behalf by Abbot John Islip on 24 January 1503, and six years later the shell of the building was complete. There is no record of the name of the architect but he is thought to have been Robert Vertue, one of the king's master masons, whose brother, William, was roofing St. George's Chapel, Windsor in a similar style at about the same time. The work was finished in 1519 during the reign of King Henry VIII, who thought at one time that he would be buried in this chapel, but in the end he joined his favourite wife, Jane Seymour, in a vault at Windsor.

*Interior of
the Chapel,
looking East*

*Bronze gates
of the
Chapel*

The architecture is in the late Perpendicular style, with a magnificent fan-vaulted ceiling and sumptuous decoration in stone, wood and bronze. The royal origins of the chapel are marked in much of the decorative work, which includes the red rose of Lancaster, the white rose of York, the portcullis of the Beauforts, the lion of England, the Welsh dragon, the greyhound of Richmond and the fleur-de-lis. Some of these royal emblems are also to be found in the fine bronze gates at the entrance which were almost certainly made by the same craftsmen as were responsible for the screen of Henry VII's tomb. Originally the windows were filled with painted glass of superb quality, but these were destroyed during the Civil War of 1642-46.

The oak stalls on either side of the chapel are intricately carved and have tall canopies. Some of these stalls go back to the time of the earlier chapel and were intended for use by the monks when they worshipped in this part of the Abbey; others were added later for use by members of the Order of the Bath. High above the stalls, and immediately below the upper windows, is a remarkable collection of statues of saints. Once there were 107 figures, now there are 95, and these represent one of the largest and best collections of late mediaeval statues in England.

The first person to be buried in the chapel was King Henry VII's wife, Elizabeth of York, who died in 1503 soon after the foundation stone had been laid. She was buried temporarily in a side-chapel until the building was ready for her to be interred in a royal tomb. Henry himself died in 1509 and was buried alongside his queen after a magnificent funeral service. Before his death he had given detailed instructions for a tomb and this was entrusted to Pietro Torrigiani, of Florence, who had been a pupil of Michelangelo and is said to have been responsible for the great artist's broken nose. The tomb, with its recumbent effigies of Henry and Elizabeth in gilt bronze, and medallions representing the Virgin Mary

Statues of saints in King Henry VII's Chapel

and the king's ten patron saints, is a masterpiece of Renaissance sculpture. Buried in the same vault is King James I, who died in 1625 and whose accession to the throne in 1603 brought about the union of England and Scotland.

Beneath the floor of the chapel are extensive vaults in which lie the bodies of King Edward VI (1537-53), Queen Mary I (1516-58), Mary, Queen of Scots (1542-87), Queen Elizabeth I (1533-1603), King Charles II (1630-85), King William III (1650-1702), Queen Mary II (1662-94), Queen Anne (1665-1714) and King George II (1683-1760), and many royal princes and princesses.

The small chapel at the east end of the main chapel is dedicated to the memory of members of the Royal Air Force who were killed in the Battle of Britain in 1940. The painted windows portray some of the pilots who took part in that battle, and also the badges of all the fighter squadrons involved in it. A roll of honour contains the names of 1,495 men and women who were killed and just below the window is a hole in the stonework made by a German bomb which fell nearby during the Battle of Britain.

Since 1725 the Chapel of King Henry VII has been the chapel of the Most Honourable Order of the Bath. This Order of Chivalry goes back to the Middle Ages

Royal Air Force Chapel and Battle of Britain window

Procession of the Order of the Bath — the painting by Canaletto (top)

The Coronation Chair.

but for several centuries it existed only on a casual basis — knights being created, generally at the Tower of London, for a particular purpose, such as a Coronation. By the end of the seventeenth century it was more or less forgotten. King George I, however, decided to reconstitute the Order and organise it on a regular basis in 1725 and the installation of knights took place in the chapel with great ceremony until 1813. There followed another century in which no installations took place, until King George V re-instituted the ceremony in 1913.

The name of the Order is derived from the ancient practice of ceremonial bathing before the reception of knighthood. The 34 senior members of the Order (Knights Grand Cross), who are mainly distinguished military leaders, together with a few highly-placed civil servants and diplomats, are installed at a colourful ceremony which takes place every four years. The Grand Master of the Order, the Prince of Wales, presides over the ceremony and the knights have personal banners hung over their stalls.

The chapel is in frequent use for celebrations of the Holy Communion and for weddings, and it also houses the Abbey's font for Baptisms.

A HOUSE OF KINGS

From its earliest days Westminster Abbey has been a place of royal crowning, and since 1066 all but two of England's monarchs have been crowned in the Abbey.

The Coronation Chair was made in 1301 on the orders of King Edward I and was designed to enclose within it the Stone of Scone which he had captured from the Scots in 1296. Made of oak, at a cost of 100 shillings, the chair was elaborately carved and painted, but during the seventeenth and eighteenth centuries most of the decorative work was broken off and visitors to the Abbey were not only allowed to sit in the chair, but were also left free to carve their initials on it.

The Stone of Scone which used to lie enclosed within the Coronation Chair is a block of rough sandstone with iron rings attached, suggesting that it was once

The Coronation of Queen Elizabeth II

carried from place to place on a pole. The earliest firm evidence concerning the stone dates from 1249 when King Alexander III of Scotland is known to have been seated on it at his Coronation in the Abbey of Scone, near Perth. But there is a strong tradition that the stone was placed in a monastrey at Scone in 846 and that all the Scottish kings were crowned on it up to the time of its seizure by the English. Various legends have identified the stone with that on which, according to the Biblical story, Jacob slept at Bethel, and the one on which St. Columba laid his head and died at Iona in 597. In 1950 it was stolen by Scottish nationalists and taken to Scotland where it remained for three months before being recovered. It was returned to Scotland by the British Government in 1996.

Throughout the Middle Ages, and until 1831, the Coronation ceremonies began in Westminster Hall, across the road from the Abbey and now forming part of the Parliament buildings. Here the Sovereign was placed on a marble throne by the Great Officers of State, who then sent a message to the Archbishop of Canterbury, waiting in the Abbey, asking him to consecrate, invest and crown the new monarch. The Dean and Canons of Westminster carried the Regalia from the Abbey to the Hall, and the king or queen was led in procession to the Abbey for the main ceremonies.

This part of the procedure was abandoned after the Coronation of King William IV, but the Dean and Canons still carry the Regalia within the Abbey at the beginning of a Coronation. The present Regalia was

King Henry V's Coronation — a stone carving on the wall of the Chantry Chapel (top)

A cope worn at the Coronation of King Charles II (bottom)

made for the Coronation of King Charles II in 1660, after the mediaeval items had been broken up and sold during Cromwell's Commonwealth.

Before the Coronation service begins, the Coronation Chair is brought from its normal place near the shrine of St. Edward the Confessor and placed in the sanctuary, facing the High Altar. At the crossing between the choir and the sanctuary a large stage-like structure is erected, and in the centre of this "theatre" a second throne is mounted on five steps. The interior of the Abbey is transformed by the building of viewing boxes and galleries for the huge congregation.

The Coronation service has four main parts:

1. *The Introduction:* The Sovereign moves in procession from the Great West Door of the Abbey to the singing of the traditional anthem "I was glad when they said unto me, "We will go into the House of the Lord". This is punctuated by cries of "Vivat Rex" or "Vivat Regina" from the scholars of Westminster School. The Archbishop of Canterbury then presents the Sovereign to the congregation on the south, west and north sides of the "theatre" and they acknowledge him or her as their "undoubted" king or queen. The Sovereign responds with a solemn promise to govern the people according to the laws of the country.

2. *The Anointing:* The Sovereign now moves to the Coronation Chair for the most solemn part of the service in which he or she is anointed by the Archbishop with holy oil on head, hands and breast. This takes place under a canopy held by four Knights of the Garter, and the choir sings the anthem "Zadok the priest" — a reminder of the anointing of the ancient Israelite kings. The oil is contained in a golden eagle and poured into a spoon through its beak.

3. *The Investiture and Crowning:* The Sovereign is next vested in a long white linen robe and another garment made of cloth of gold. A sword and spurs are then affixed, a stole is draped around the neck, and

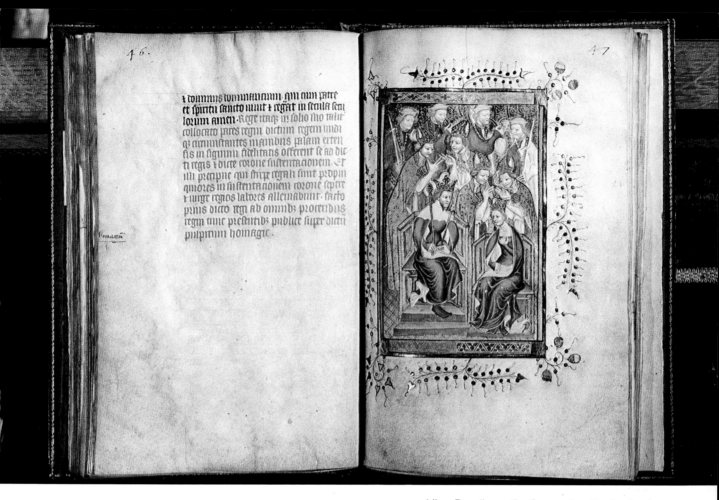

Liber Regalis — *the Coronation Service book*

the vestments are completed with a four-cornered cloak. An Orb is now presented and this is followed by the Ring. Next comes the Sceptre, a symbol of royal power and justice, and this is balanced in the other hand by the Rod with a Dove, symbolising equity and mercy. Finally, the Archbishop places the Crown of St. Edward on the Sovereign's head — an action which is followed immediately by acclamations from the people, fanfares of trumpets, and the firing of guns outside.

4. *The Enthroning and Homage:* The Sovereign leaves the Coronation Chair and goes to the throne in the "theatre" where he or she receives the homage of representatives of the Bishops and the Peers, and a three-fold acclamation from the people present.

In the case of a king, his consort is then crowned as queen in a simpler ceremony, but there is no ceremony for the husband of a female Sovereign. William III and Mary II are the only king and queen to have held the English throne jointly and a companion Coronation Chair (now in the Abbey museum) was made for their Coronation in 1689.

The present Coronation Service may be traced to the service used by St. Dunstan at the Coronation of King Edgar at Bath in 973, and this in turn was based on earlier services. During the Middle Ages the service became highly elaborate, reaching its most developed form in the late fourteenth century. In the Library of Westminster Abbey there is a copy of *Liber Regalis* (the King's Book) containing the service used at the Coronation of the boy-king Richard II in 1377. This beautiful, illuminated book was used at subsequent Coronations until the service was translated from Latin into English for the Coronation of James I in 1603, and eventually discarded by James II in 1685. Since 1689 there have been only minor changes, and the main difference in the twentieth century Coronations is to be found in their careful organisation and the precision of the ceremonial now seen by hundreds of millions of people by means of television.

A ROYAL REFORMER

Queen Elizabeth I, whose reign (1558-1603) is generally regarded as the most brilliant in English history, came to the throne in troubled times. This was reflected both in the circumstances of her Coronation and in the life of the Abbey in which she was crowned.

During the early days of 1540, when the English Reformation was gathering pace, the Benedictine monastery at Westminster was dissolved on the orders of King Henry VIII who had embarked upon the suppression of all the religious houses in the country. Secular priests took the place of the monks and from 1550 to 1560 the Abbey was the cathedral of a newly-created diocese of Westminster. This diocese was re-absorbed into the diocese of London in 1560 and for the next six years the Abbey and St. Paul's were both regarded as London cathedrals. It was during this time that some of Westminster Abbey's revenues were used to finance the repair of St. Paul's — hence the saying "Robbing Peter to pay Paul".

In 1556 Queen Mary I restored England's relations with Rome and re-established a small community of Benedictine monks at Westminster. But this return to the old order was shortlived for Mary died in 1558 and was succeeded by Elizabeth, her half-sister, who was committed to England's independence and to the reform of the church.

Elizabeth was crowned in the Abbey on 15 January 1559. The ceremony was carried out, partly in Latin and partly in English, by the Bishop of Carlisle, Dr. Owen Oglethorpe, as the Archbishopric of Canterbury was vacant and the Archbishop of York, along with most of the other bishops, refused to be involved. The new Queen, who had been warmly welcomed by large crowds while on her way to the Abbey, was not altogether happy about her Coronation, which seemed to her to contain too many ceremonies from the unreformed past. She complained that the oil used for her anointing "stank" and when the Host was elevated at the Holy Communion she retired from the scene for a time.

On 21 May in the following year the monks finally departed from the Abbey, which ceased to be a monastery and was designated the Collegiate Church of St. Peter in Westminster. A Royal Charter, which was never actually signed by Queen Elizabeth, decreed that the church should be governed by a Dean, supported by twelve Prebendaries. There should also be an Upper Master and an Usher for the school, and 40 scholars, "besides ministers, singers and organists, ten queristers and twelve poor soldiers". The foundation of the school, now the

Tomb of Queen Elizabeth I and Queen Mary I

Westminster School and the Victoria Tower of the House of Lords (top)

The Essex ring (bottom)

famous Westminster School with some 600 pupils, was an important element in the new arrangement. The monastic granary became the school dormitory and the monks' dormitory became the schoolroom, where all the teaching was given.

The Charter laid down in considerable detail how the life of the Abbey and the school should be ordered, and its provisions still provide the framework of the Abbey's life today. The Dean and four Canons (successors of the Prebendaries) are appointed by the Sovereign, on the advice of the Prime Minister, and form a corporate body responsible to the Crown for the Abbey's affairs. They are assisted by a staff of over 150 other, mainly lay, people.

For most of its pre-Reformation life Westminster Abbey had been one of the European monasteries exempted by the Pope from local episcopal authority. Queen Elizabeth I continued this exemption, reserving authority over the Abbey to herself — as Visitor. This is the position today. The Collegiate Church of St. Peter in Westminster is a "Royal Peculiar", in no way subject to the authority, or within the jurisdiction, of any bishop or archbishop. The Bishop of London and the Archbishop of Canterbury attend the Abbey on certain occasions, and take part in its services, but always as guests (except on the day of a Coronation) and never with authority.

As King Edward the Confessor is regarded as the founder of Westminster Abbey, so is Queen Elizabeth I regarded as the foundress of the present Collegiate Church. When she died in 1603 it was natural that she should be buried in the Abbey and her body was laid to rest in the north aisle of the Chapel of King Henry VII, where Queen Mary I had been interred almost half a century earlier and been left without a tomb.

Queen Elizabeth's fine monument, with its recumbent effigy portraying the great Tudor queen in her latter years, was erected by King James I and completed in 1606. The coffins of the two queen lie above each other and King James, well aware of their enmity in life, was inspired to provide a Latin inscription which read: "Consorts both in throne and grave, here rest we two sisters, Elizabeth and Mary, in the hope of one resurrection".

Among those who lost their lives, for a variety of reasons, during the turbulent Reformation era, was Robert Devereux, Earl of Essex. A close friend of the Queen, she gave him a ring and told him to send it to her if ever he needed her help. When imprisoned in the Tower of London and under sentence of death, the Earl despatched the ring to the Queen but, for some unknown reason, it never reached her and he was beheaded. In 1927 the Dean and Chapter were presented with what is believed to be this ring — a gold band with a cameo portrait of Queen Elizabeth — which is now displayed in the Abbey museum.

Queen Elizabeth I in her Coronation robes

A HOLY AND MUCH LOVED LADY

One of the most attractive people to be associated with Westminster Abbey over the course of its long history is Lady Margaret Beaufort. In his sermon at her funeral, Bishop John Fisher of Rochester, who had been Lady Margaret's friend and confessor and was himself to be canonised as a saint, said, "Everyone that knew her loved her, and everything that she said or did became her".

Born in 1443, Lady Margaret was, as a small child, married to the Earl of Suffolk. At the age of 13 she was married again, this time to Edmund Tudor, Earl of Richmond, and a year later she bore a child — the future King Henry VII. Following the death of Edmund Tudor, she married Lord Henry Stafford, son of the Duke of Buckingham, and when he died she married Thomas, Lord Stanley, who became Earl of Derby.

Lady Margaret was a frequent visitor to the Abbey and encouraged her son to rebuild the Lady Chapel. She endowed a number of charities connected to this chapel, one of which — for poor widows — still ex-

ists. The records of the Cellarer mention a visit by Lady Margaret in 1501 to inspect the "new work". This was probably the almshouse which she founded just outside the monastery, west of the present Dean's Yard, and the Cellarer notes the expenditure of money on cleaning the Horse Pool nearby, and the planting of twenty elm trees.

Her patronage extended also to the realm of education and she is remembered in Cambridge as the foundress of Christ's and St. John's colleges. She endowed Chairs of Divinity at Oxford and Cambridge which still bear her name. A woman of deep devotion, Lady Margaret died in the Abbot's House at Westminster on 29 June 1509, and her personal prayer book is now in the Abbey Library.

The tomb of Lady Margaret, in the Chapel of King Henry VII, is the work of Pietro Torrigiani and is another masterpiece of early Renaissance sculpture in gilt bronze. She is portrayed in a widow's dress and particularly striking are her wrinkled hands, joined in prayer. The iron grille around the tomb was originally gilded and was sold in 1823, but it was later recovered from a country house and replaced in 1915.

An illustrated page from Lady Margaret Beaufort's prayer book

The Tomb of Lady Margaret Beaufort

HAVENS OF PEACE AND PRAYER

All the mediaeval churches incorporated small chapels within their main structure, and the large cathedrals and abbeys had many of these chapels. They served several purposes. Where there were a lot of priests, and it was the custom for each priest to say Mass every day, the chapels enabled several services to be held at the same time. For small congregations it was obviously preferable, then as now, to gather at the altar of a chapel rather than in the great open spaces at the high altar or the nave altar. Sometimes chapels were built to honour a particular saint and in hope of obtaining the benefit of the saint's prayers. Chantry chapels were designed as the burial place of important people and provision was made for a priest to say Mass in them every day for the repose of the soul of the person buried there.

Westminster Abbey was intended to have a large number of chapels in use, but at the Reformation the altars, statues and other beautiful furnishings in them were destroyed, and during the seventeenth and eighteenth centuries they were gradually filled with tombs and monuments. More recently, however, some of the chapels have been restored and brought back into regular use — generally for celebrations of the Holy Communion on weekdays, but also for Weddings, Confirmations, Confessions and private prayer. When the Abbey is crowded with pilgrims and tourists, the chapels are welcome havens of peace.

Chapel of St. Faith

Built during the second half of the thirteenth century, as part of King Henry III's great rebuilding scheme, this chapel lies at the southern end of the south transept and is regarded by many people as the most evocative place in the entire Abbey. On the east wall, above the altar, is a fine painting of St. Faith, dating back to at least 1265 and perhaps the first decoration to be added to the rebuilt Abbey. It has been described as "the most romantic painting in London" and portrays St. Faith holding a gridiron — the symbol of her third century martyrdom by burning. On the lower

left of the saint is a figure of a Benedictine monk in prayer. At the base of the chapel's ceiling ribs are a series of carved heads, also dating from the mid-thirteenth century and including one with negroid features.

Chapel of St. George

Sometimes known as the Warriors' Chapel, and occupying the south west corner of the nave, not far from the Tomb of the Unknown Warrior, this chapel was reconstructed and dedicated in 1932 in memory of the men and women who were killed in the First World War. It was designed by a distinguished architect and artist, Sir Ninian Comper, and the fine metalwork is a reminder of the churches of Spain. Hanging within the chapel is the so-called ''Padre's flag''. This blood-stained flag was used by an army chaplain from 1914-18 as an altar cloth and also to cover the bodies of dead soldiers at the time of their burial. It covered the coffin of the Unknown Warrior at the time of his burial in the Abbey in 1920. The chapel also contains a bust of William Booth, the founder of the Salvation Army.

Chapel fo King Henry V

When King Henry V died in 1422, there was no room for another tomb in the Chapel of St. Edward, so strong had been the belief of his predecessors that burial in close proximity to the body of the saint would have eternal advantages. The great warrior king had, however, forseen the likelihood of his being excluded from these advantages, so in his will he left precise instructions that he should be buried at the eastern entrance to St. Edward's Chapel and that a chantry chapel should be built above his head, high in the apse of the Abbey. His wishes were carried out by an ingenious architect, John Thirske, who not only contrived to create a chapel with room for about 20 people, but also incorporated into it a great deal of fine sculpture in stone which is an adornment of the Abbey as a whole.

Alabaster figure in the Chapel of Our Lady of Pew

Islip Chantry Chapel — upper storey

Chapel of Our Lady of Pew

Near the Islip Chapel and at the entrance to the Chapel of St. John Baptist, which is now occupied by tombs, is what appears at first sight to be a vestibule. This is in fact the tiny Chapel of Our Lady of Pew, established in 1376 when Dame Mary de St. Pol, widow of Aymer de Valence, Earl of Pembroke, presented the Abbey with an alabaster figure of the Blessed Virgin Mary. This figure disappeared during the turmoil of the sixteenth century but was replaced by a modern alabaster figure of the Virgin and Child in 1971. The painted vaulting on the low ceiling of the chapel offers a glimpse of what the whole of the mediaeval Abbey was like, in its resplendent colours. There is a beautiful ceiling boss of the Assumption dating from the second half of the fourteenth century.

Islip Chantry Chapel

John Islip was the last of the great Abbots of Westminster and died only eight years before the monastery was dissolved by King Henry VIII. During this time as Abbot (1500-1532) the nave of the Abbey was completed and also the rebuilding of the Lady Chapel. He planned a central tower which never materialised, but he built a chapel with two storeys in the north ambulatory. Known as the Jesus Chapel, it has an altar on each floor, and when Abbot Islip died at his country manor in 1532 he was brought back to Westminster to be buried in this chapel. His tomb slab is now the altar in the upper story chapel which was furnished in 1950 as a memorial to the nurses who were killed during the Second World War. The bronze crucifix is the duplicate of an original in the Church of Ss. Annunziata in Florence.

MEMORIES AND MONUMENTS

No fewer than 32 Sovereigns or their consorts are buried within the walls of Westminster Abbey, and also many more of their relatives, some of whom were given large and beautiful tombs.

On the north side of the sanctuary lies Edmund Crouchback, who was Earl of Lancaster in the thirteenth century and a son of King Henry III. As befits a warrior, his effigy portrays him in mail armour; above him is a triple canopy. Near Edmund is the tomb of his first wife, Aveline, who died in 1274 and was very beautiful as well as exceedingly rich. Their wedding was the first to be held in the Abbey after King Henry II's rebuilding and her tomb is intricately carved.

From the same period, and placed between the tombs of Edmund and Aveline, is the magnificent tomb of Aymer de Valence, Earl of Pembroke, who played a prominent part in the wars against Scotland in the early fourteenth century and eventually died while on an embassy in France. Like Crouchback, he is portrayed in armour and on the canopy he is shown on horseback.

The most touching tombs and monuments in the Abbey are those of children. In the Chapel of St. Edmund there are tiny alabaster effigies of William of Windsor and Blanche of the Tower — children of King Edward III who died in infancy in the fourteenth century. Not far from the tomb of Queen Elizabeth I, in the Chapel of King Henry VII, in what is sometimes called "The Innocents' Corner", are monuments to two daughters of King James I. Princess Sophia, who died only three days after her birth in 1606, is portrayed in a cradle, while her sister, Princess Mary, who died in the following year, aged two years, is shown reclining on her elbow.

Tombs of Aveline of Lancaster, Aymer de Valence and Edmund of Lancaster

Monument to Lady Burghley and the Countess of Oxford (1589)

Monument to Lord and Lady Bourgchier (1430)

Near these children is a sarcophagus containing the bones of two boys — discovered in the Tower of London and believed to be those of King Edward V and his brother, Richard, who are said to have been murdered in 1483 on the instructions of their uncle, King Richard III.

In the south aisle of the Chapel of King Henry VII is the magnificent tomb of Mary, Queen of Scots, who was a claimant to the English throne during the reign of Queen Elizabeth I. She was captured in 1568 and after 19 years in prison was beheaded, then buried in Peterborough Cathedral. When King James I succeeded Elizabeth in 1603 he ordered that Mary — who was his mother — should be brought to Westminster Abbey. The white marble effigy shows her in a long mantle and a lace ruff; at her feet is the Scottish lion with a crown.

The Chapel of St. Nicholas contains several fine Elizabethan monuments, including a large one erected by Lord Burghley to commemorate his wife, Mildred Cecil, and his daughter, Anne, Countess of Oxford, who died within a year of each other in 1588-89. Nearby, mounted on a pyramid of black and white marble, is a vase containing the heart of Anne Sophia who was the infant daughter of the French Ambassador in London and died in 1605.

The largest monument in the Abbey is that of Henry, Baron Hunsdon who was in charge of Queen Elizabeth's personal bodyguard at the time of the Spanish Armada and died in 1596. Erected in the Chapel of St. John Baptist, this monument is 36 feet high and is a colourful mixture of marble, gilt and heraldic devices. Another large, but much less attractive, monument stands nearby in the north ambulatory and commemorates James Wolfe — the British general who captured Quebec from the French and was killed in 1759 at the age of 32. The monument portrays Wolfe receiving a laurel wreath and the palm of victory from an angel at the time of his death. These are but a few of some hundreds of tombs and monuments in Westminster Abbey. The presence of so many of them undoubtedly makes it more difficult

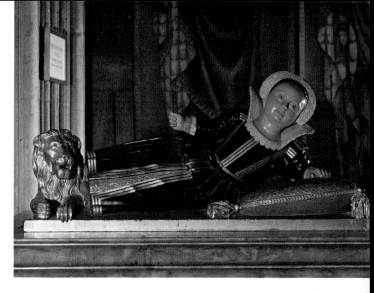

Effigy of Princess Mary

to see and appreciate the architecture of the building at its lower levels, but they remind worshippers and visitors of the Abbey's intimate links with English history and of the host of people who have contributed in some way to the life of the nation across the centuries.

Tomb of Margaret, Countess of Lennox (1578). Her son, Lord Darnley, married Mary, Queen of Scots, and is portrayed on the tomb with a crown above his head.

An artist's reconstruction of Westminster Abbey during
the late Middle Ages when it was a Benedictine
monastery

THE MONASTIC CENTURIES

When King Edward the Confessor decided to build a
new monastery for the monks who were living on the
Isle of Thorns in the eleventh century this religious
community, which had been installed by St. Dunstan,
was living according to the Rule of St. Benedict. The
Rule, which still governs the life of the Benedictine
Order, was drawn up by St. Benedict in the sixth cen-
tuty and emphasises the priority of worship — expres-
sed in regular daily services and integrated with a
routine of work, study and private prayer. The monks
make life -long vows involving celibacy, the sharing of
possessions and obedience to an elected abbot.
Benedict, who was canonised as a saint after his
death, established twelve monasteries in Italy and his
movement grew rapidly during the Middle Ages when

the "black monks", as they were often called because
of their black robes, made an important contribution
to European civilisation. They became deeply invoved
in education and many of England's great cathedrals
were originally Benedictine monasteries.
A mediaeval monastery closely resembled a village
community. At Westminster there were rarely more
than 50 monks, even when the religious life was most
popular, and sometimes there were only about 30, es-
pecially when outbreaks of plague had taken their toll.
But in addition to the monks there were perhaps as
many as 300 other people involved in the life of the
monastery. Stonemasons, carpenters and plumbers
were needed during the times of building or reconstruction. Servants were employed both inside and
outside the buildings. The school attracted boys from
the immediate neighbourhood and beyond. Chari-

table work drew in beggars and paupers. Provision was made for elderly people and former servants of the Community.

At Westminster, as elsewhere, the monastery consisted of a number of different buildings, dominated by the great church in which the monks assembled seven times a day for worship. The territory was some what larger than the present precincts and the monks owned land in other parts of London, besides 216 manors in other parts of the country. A high wall separated the monastery from the outside world, and large sections of the fourteenth century wall are still to be seen, enclosing the garden of the present Abbey. This garden, which is open to visitors on Thursdays, is believed to be the oldest in England, having been under continuous cultivation for over 900 years. In addition to growing fruit, vegetables and herbs, the monks had an oyster bed, served by the tidal Thames. The open space, now grassed and known as Dean's Yard, was formerly the monastery farmyard. Here there was a granary, stables and other farm buildings. The Guestmaster, who was responsible for entertaining the Abbey's visitors, and the Cellarer, who looked after the general provisioning of the monastery, also had their quarters in this area — not far from the main gate.

St. Benedict

Tomb of Abbot Simon de Langham

The East Cloister

In mediaeval times, the Great Cloiser — now a pleasant place for strolling visitors — was a hive of activity. It was in effect a series of long rooms, for the windows were filled with glass, the walls were painted and hung with pictures, lamps were suspended from the roof, and the floor was strewn with rushes.

The north walk, built in the time of King Henry III, was a reading and writing room. At each end was a large bookcase, with smaller ones attached to the walls, and beneath the windows were small compartments, each equipped with a table and seat where the monks could study. The west walk, built by Abbot Litlyngton in the fourteenth century, was the place for education. Here the Novice Master instructed the younger monks, and children came for tuition in a variety of religious and secular subjects. The south walk, which has the tombs of three twelfth and thirteenth-century abbots, led to the Refectory where the monks had their meals. Unfortunately, this important Norman building was destroyed when the monastery was dissolved in the sixteenth century.

The east walk leads to the Chapter House — a magnificent building erected in the middle of the thirteenth century, of octagonal shape, with a graceful central column supporting the great vaulted roof. The thirteenth century floor, is in near-perfect condition, having been covered with wooden boards for several centuries. Here the monks met every day after the celebration of Mass in order to transact the business of the monastery and to receive instructions about their daily duties. It is the largest Chapter House in England, apart from that at Lincoln, and its size is due

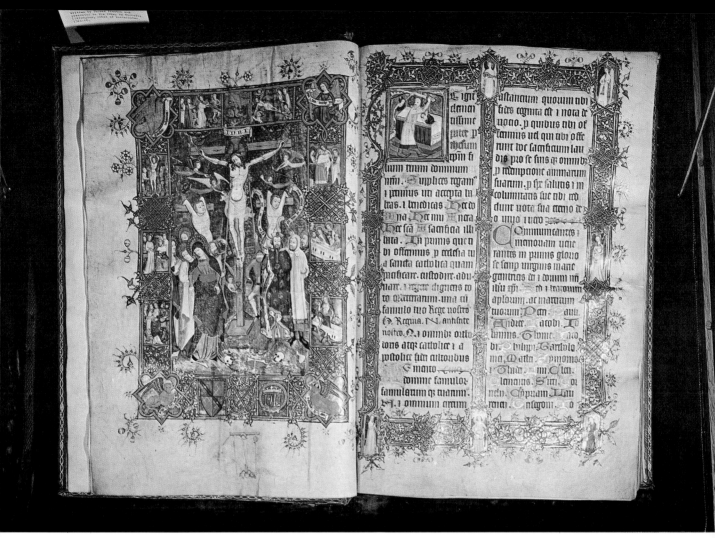

The Litlyngton Missal

to the fact that is was intended for secular as well as monastic use. From the second half of the thirteenth century until the end of the reign of King Henry VIII in the middle of the sixteenth century it was used for meetings of the House of Commons. This is why it has been in the hands of the Crown, not of the Dean and Chapter, since the monastery was dissolved.

Near the entrance to the Chapter House is a door leading to the former monks' dormitory. This was originally a huge chamber, 173 feet long, with a fine hammer-beam roof dating from the end of the fifteenth century. The monks usually went to bed at about 8 p.m., after the service of Compline, but they were roused again at 2 a.m. for the night Office. Part of the staircase from the dormitory to the church can still be seen high up in the south transept of the Abbey.

The Chapter House — interior

The Chapter Library, formerly the Monks' Dormitory

After the dissolution of the monastery, the dormitory was divided in half — one part being used as the school room of Westminster School and the other turned into the present Chapter Library. The school-room, which eventually became the main asssembly hall of the enlarged public school, was destroyed by incendiary bombs in the Second World War, but the Chapter Library has changed little since it was established by Dean Williams in the seventeenth century. Among its treasures are the Litlyngton Missal, a beautifully illuminated service book, written and illustrated in the fourteenth century by a scribe who stayed on to become a monk of Westminster.

Just a few feet from the Library entrance are the massive doors of the Chapel of the Pyx. This vaulted chamber was built sometime between 1065 and 1090 and was used as a chapel in the Middle Ages. It was also the treasury of the monastery and may have been the place where the Coronation Regalia was kept. For many years the pyx, or box, containing the standard pieces of gold and silver for testing the coinage of the realm was kept here.

The Dark Cloister, with its heavy barrel-shaped roof dating from the eleventh century, leads to the Little Cloister — one of the most delightful parts of the Abbey's precincts, with its seventeenth century arches and a lively fountain. This was originally the monastic Infirmary to which monks were sent when ill or old, or simply in need of rest. A decorated doorway of the fourteenth century leads to the Chapel of St. Catherine — now a ruin but clearly recognisable as the remains of a large twelfth century church.

Jerusalem Chamber

As in the case of the Chapter House, the Chapel of St. Catherine was designed for more than monastic use and during the Middle Ages the consecration of bishops often took place here, as well as other ecclesiastical assemblies. In 1176 when a dispute arose as to whether the Archbishop of Canterbury had precedence over the Archbishop of York, a synod was convened in the chapel and presided over by a Papal Legate. The Archbishop of Canterbury arrived in the chapel first and sat on the right hand of the Legate. The Archbishop of York refused to occupy the left hand seat and instead sat on Canterbury's knee. A brawl developed among the supporters of the two archbishops, in the course of which York's cope was torn; whereupon King Henry II, who was attending Mass in the Abbey, was called to settle the matter. The king announced that henceforth the Archbishop of York would have the title "Primate of England" — and the Archbishop of Canterbury the title "Primate of All England" — titles which have remained to the present day.

It was in this chapel, also, that King Henry III, surrounded by bishops and archbishops, and with a Gospel in one hand and a lighted candle in the other, swore to maintain the rights of the English people enshrined in the Magna Carta.

The houses in this part of the precincts were built at the end of the seventeenth century, but some of them were badly damaged during air raids on London in 1941 and had to rebuilt after the war. They are occupied by the clergy of the Abbey and other officers of the Collegiate body.

For the greater part of the Middle Ages the Abbot of Westminster held high office in the state as well as responsibility for his monastic community. It was therefore convenient for him to live near the Great Gate of the monastery where he could entertain important guests without disturbing the life of the community and also play his part in state affairs.

The earliest abbots appear to have had their lodgings near the western entrance to the Great Cloister, and it was on this site that Abbot Nicholas de Litlyngton rebuilt the Abbot's lodging on a palatial scale in the latter part of the fourteenth century. Ater the dissolution of the monastery, the Abbot's lodging became the Deanery and this was described by Professor Lethaby as "the most perfect, and indeed the only approximately complete, mediaeval house now existing in London, and it has special beauties which must always have been exceptional". In 1941 incendiary bombs set fire to the roof and much of the house was completely destroyed. Fortunately the most historic rooms were undamaged and are still in use.

Of these rooms two are of special importance. The Jerusalem Chamber, designed as the Abbot's drawing room, was completed in about 1370 and the fine, painted roof bears the monograms of Abbot Litlyngton and Richard II, who was king at that time. It was common for monastic rooms to be named after Biblical sites or themes, and adjoining the Jerusalem Chamber are two other rooms — Jericho and Samaria.

On 20 March 1413, King Henry IV, who had come to pray at the Shrine of St. Edward before embarking upon an expedition to the Holy Land, had a stroke and was carried into the Jerusalem Chamber to lie before the fire. The scene has been described, probably with generous use of the imagination, by a contemporary chronicler who records that when the king recovered slightly he asked where he was. On being told that he was in the chamber named Jerusalem, he said "Laud be to the Father of Heaven, for now I know that I shall die in this chamber, according to the prophecy made of me beforesaid, that I should die in Jerusalem". Soon afterwards he died, and according to Shakespeare, who has immortalised the event in his play Henry IV, Prince Hal — about to become King Henry V — tried on the crown while his father was still alive and was rebuked for his pains.

The chamber has also passed into history because of its special association with the English Bible. The committee responsible for the Authorised Version of the Bible, published in 1611, met regularly in the chamber, as did those who worked on the Revised Version (1881-85) and the New English Bible (1961-70). Between 1643 and 1649 the Westminster Assembly of Divines held 1,163 sessions here and in 1646 completed the Westminster Confession of Faith, which is the definitive statement of Presbyterian doctrine in the English-speaking world.

In 1624 Dean John Williams entertained in the chamber the French Ambassador who had been involved in arranging the betrothal of the Prince of Wales, soon to become King Charles I, to Princess Henrietta Maria. Although the occasion was not, it seems, a very successful one, Dean Williams erected the present cedarwood overmantel, with carved heads of the Prince and Princess, to mark the event. During the eighteenth century, when burials in the Abbey usually took place at night, the bodies of many famous people, including those of Joseph Addison and Isaac Newton, lay in state in the chamber.

The Dean and Chapter have for many years held their regular meetings to conduct the business of the Abbey in the chamber, and the Regalia is kept here on the night before a Coronation.

Soon after the completion of the Jerusalem Chamber, Abbot Litlyngton began to build a great dining hall adjoining the chamber, and this was finished about 1376. It remains substantially unaltered, though a minstrels' gallery was added at the end of the sixteenth century. There is a fine timbered roof and the tables are said to have been made from the ships of the Spanish Armada wrecked on English shores. After the dissolution of the monastery, it became known as College Hall and is now used mainly by the pupils of Westminster School, though it remains the property of Dean and Chapter who use it occasionally for entertaining guests.

The final years of the monastery are a sad story. John Islip, the last of the great Abbots of Westminster, died in 1532. After a long vacancy he was succeeded, not by a Westminster monk elected by the rest of the community, according to custom, but by a royal nominee — William Boston, a monk of Peterborough. Boston proved to be a pliant instrument in the hands of King Henry VIII who was determined to suppress all the monasteries and seize their property. The administration of the Abbey was neglected and discipline became lax. Nothing scandalous was ever alleged against the Community, but on 16 January 1540 Abbot Boston and 24 monks assembled in the Chapter House to sign a Deed of Surrender. Everything of material value went to the king and much of the Abbey's artistic heritage was destroyed. A Benedictine community was re-established at

Grave of an Abbey plumber (top)

Grave of the Unknown Warrior (centre)

Memorial to Sir Winston Churchill (bottom)

Westminster towards the end of 1556, under a new Abbot, John de Feckenham, and soon there were 50 monks in residence. But the death of Queen Mary I two years later signalled the end of this brief revival and a few months after Queen Elizabeth's Coronation in 1559 the monastery was finally dissolved. The monks had gone for good.

THE GREAT AND THE SMALL

During the middle Ages burial in Westminster Abbey was, with very few exceptions, confined to kings and queens, members of royal families, and eventually abbots of Westminster. Monks were generally buried in the cloisters or elsewhere in the precincts.

Today, however, about 2,500 people have graves or memorials in the Abbey and, although it has certainly become a "Temple of Fame", there are still many reminders of quite ordinary people to be seen on gravestones and memorial plaques. Decisions about burial or memorialisation in the Abbey lie with the Dean. In practice, the Dean consults his colleagues, the Canons, and in the case of public figures more widely, but the decision is his alone. The tradition that members of the Abbey community should be buried in the church or the precincts continues.

It was Queen Elizabeth I who opened the Abbey to the burial of people not of royal blood but, as the fine monuments in the apse chapels indicate, the honour was for some time restricted to prominent courtiers and members of noble families. Another 150 years were to pass before burial in the Abbey seemed appropriate for anyone, irrespective of birth or rank, who had made a notable contribution to the life of the nation and perhaps to the welfare of the human race as a whole.

The best known of all the graves in the Abbey, and the one most highly regarded, is, paradoxically, that of someone whose name is unknown. During the First World War an army chaplain conceived the idea of burying in Westminster Abbey the body of a

Memorial statues of two famous Prime Ministers — W.E. Gladstone and Sir Robert Peel — and of William Wilberforce, a social reformer and leader of the campaign which led to the abolition of the slave trade

member of the armed forces who had been killed and who would represent the multitude who had sacrificed their lives in the conflict. At first the idea was not taken very seriously, but when the war was over it was pursued vigorously by the then Dean of Westminster, Bishop Herbert Edward Ryle, and on 11 November 1920 the body of an unknown warrior was carried in solemn procession to the Abbey where, in the presence of King George V, members of the Royal Family, the Prime Minister and members of the Cabinet, and many other distinguished leaders, it was interred at the west end of the nave.

The grave contains soil from France, where so many were killed, and the slab of black marble came from a quarry in Belgium, not far from the place where the first shots of the war were fired. Today, all Heads of foreign states making official visits to London come to the Abbey soon after their arrival to lay a wreath on the Unknown Warrior's grave. This is the only spot in the Abbey on which no-one is permitted to walk.

Near this grave is a memorial to Sir Winston Churchill, Britain's famous Prime Minister in the Second World War, who died in 1965 and is buried at Bladon, near his birthplace in Oxfordshire. Not far away, on the north side of the nave, is a group of famous Socialist leaders of the twentieth century — Ramsey MacDonald and Clement Attlee, both of whom were Prime Ministers, Ernest Bevin, Trades Union leader and Foreign Secretary, and Sidney and Beatrice Webb, social thinkers and writers.

The statesmen of the nineteenth century are together in the north transept, in what is sometimes called

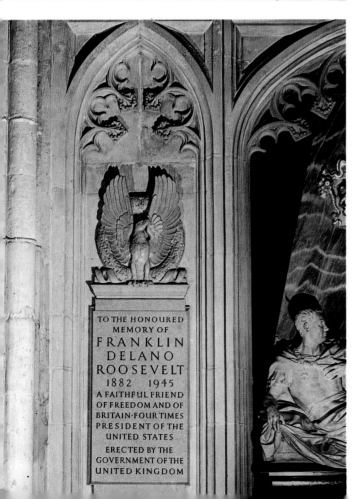

IN MEMORY, OF MR THŌ: SMITH OF ELMLY-LOVET, IN Ỹ COVNTY OF WOR= CESTER, & BACH: OF ARTS LATE OF CH: CH: OXFORD. WHO THROVGH Ỹ SPOTTED VAILE OF ᵗᴴᴱ SMALL-POX, RENDRED A PVRE, & VN= SPOTTED SOVL TO GOD. EXPECTING, BVT NOT FEARING DEATH; Wᶜᴴ ENDED HIS DAYEˢ, MARCH ᵀᴴᴱ 10ᵀᴴ ANNO DO͞M 166¾

ÆTATIS SVÆ 27.

The Virtues which in his ſhort life were ſhown, haue equalld been by few, ſurpaſſd by none

TO THE HONOURED
MEMORY OF
FRANKLIN
DELANO
ROOSEVELT
1882   1945
A FAITHFUL FRIEND
OF FREEDOM AND OF
BRITAIN·FOUR TIMES
PRESIDENT OF THE
UNITED STATES
ERECTED BY THE
GOVERNMENT OF THE
UNITED KINGDOM

"Statesmen's Aisle". Here there are statues of Robert Peel, W.E. Gladstone, Benjamín Disraeli, George Canning and Viscount Palmerston — all Prime Ministers during the time of Britain's greatest imperial power. Towering over them is a huge monument to William Pitt, 1st Earl of Chatham, who was twice Prime Minister in the eighteenth century and, having first been buried in Kent, was disinterred and re-buried in the Abbey at the request of Parliament in the reign of King George III.

Another statesman to be disinterred was Oliver Cromwell, Lord Protector during the Commonwealth, who was buried at the east end of the Chapel of King Henry VII in 1658, only to be exhumed two years later in order that his body might be dragged through the streets of London in disgrace.

The burial of Sir Isaac Newton, the mathematician and philosopher, at the east end of the nave in 1727, and the erection of a monument to him on the choir screen a few years later, opened the way to the burial and memorialisation of a number of famous scientists. Within a few feet of Newton's grave is that of William Herschel, the pioneer of modern astronomy and discoverer of the planet Uranus, who died in 1822. His son, John Herschel, who was also a distinguished astronomer and mathematician, lies near him.

The grave of Charles Darwin is a surprise to some visitors, since his theory of evolution by natural selection, advanced in his book *The Origin of Species* (1859), is often thought to have undermined the Christian faith. Pioneer work in the field of modern atomic physics is represented in the memorials to John Joseph Thomson and Ernest Rutherford.

Quite different is the memorial to Dame Grace Gethin in the south choir aisle. Dame Grace was a devout young lady who died in 1697, aged 20, and after her death a book of her private devotions was published. Her parents also endowed a charity in her memory to provide "forty sixpenny loaves of good weight for

Wax effigies of King Charles II and Horatio Nelson

twenty poor men and twenty poor women of this area, and a sermon in the Abbey on Ash Wednesday''. The sermon, for which the preacher receives a fee of £1, is still preached and her memory recalled.

The body of David Livingstone, the great nineteenth century missionary and explorer of Africa, lies in the centre of the nave, having been carried by his African servants for many months from the remote village where he died to the seaport of Zanzibar. Livingstone's funeral in the Abbey in 1874 was a great national event in Victorian England, and an African boy was brought to London to throw a palm branch into the grave.

During the Middle Ages it was customary at the funeral of an important person for a dressed effigy of the deceased to be carried in the procession and then placed on the grave until a monument was erected. The earliest of these effigies were in wood but from the seventeenth century onwards they were generally made of wax, and a collection of them, including those of King Edward III (in wood) and Queen Elizabeth I, King Charles II and Queen Anne (in wax) are on display in the Abbey museum. The effigy of Horatio Nelson, the great sailor, was placed in the Abbey in 1806, a year after his death, as a counter-attraction to his tomb in St. Paul's Cathedral which was attracting much public interest at the time.

Tomb of Geoffrey Chaucer (top)

Lease for Geoffrey Chaucer's house, near the Lady Chapel (1399) (bottom)

Memorial to George Frederick Handel

A CORNER FOR THE ARTISTS

The first representative of English literature to be buried in Westminster Abbey was Robert de Waldeby, a learned Archbishop of York and friend of the Black Prince, who died in 1397. But the establishing of what came to be known as Poets' Corner, in the south transept, was due to the burial there of Geoffrey Chaucer, "the father of English song", and later of Edmund Spenser.

The burial in the Abbey of Geoffrey Chaucer in 1400 seems to have been due not to his fame as a poet or as the author of the *Canterbury Tales,* but rather to his position as Clerk of the King's Works at the Palace of Westminster. Towards the end of his life he lived in a house near the old Lady Chapel of the Abbey and this was pulled down to make room for the Chapel of King Henry VII. Edmund Spenser, author of the *Faerie Queen* was deliberately buried near Chaucer and it is said that at his funeral in 1599 all his contemporaries, probably including Shakespeare, wrote elegies which they threw into his grave, together with the pens with which they had written them.

Ben Jonson, friend of Shakespeare and Bacon, was educated at Westminster School during the reign of Queen Elizabeth I and was appointed Poet Laureate by King James I in 1619. On his death in 1637 he was buried, allegedly standing upright, in the nave of the Abbey, where the simple inscription "O Rare Ben Jonson" is still to be seen on his gravestone. A monument with the same inscription was erected in Poets' Corner during the early part of the eighteenth century.

By this time the custom of burying or memorialising in Poets' Corner was firmly established. Shakespeare had been buried at Stratford-upon-Avon and there was talk of bringing his remains to Westminster, but in the end they were left in peace and instead he was given a monument in Poets' Corner in 1740. Around this monument there are now many other memorials to notable poets and writers.

Although Joseph Addison, the great essayist, was buried in the Chapel of King Henry VII in 1719, he had no memorial until his statue was erected in 1809. Charles Dickens, the novelist, was buried in Poets' Corner in 1870 and was followed, some 20 years later, by the poets Robert Browning and Alfred Tennyson. In recent years memorial stones have been placed in the floor to commemorate Lord Byron, T.S. Eliot, W.H. Auden, Gerard Manley Hopkins, Henry James and George Eliot.

Among all these poets and writers is the grave of George Frederick Handel, the composer, who died in 1759. On the wall, above the grave, is a statue of Handel which shows him holding a copy of the aria "I know that my Redeemer liveth" from his celebrated work *Messiah.* During the 18th century Handel's music was often heard in Westminster Abbey and at a Handel commemoration in 1784 a choir of almost 300 voices and an orchestra of 249 performed *Messiah* to an audience of 3,000 people, including King

Sarah Siddons as the "Tragic Muse" — a painting by Sir Joshua Reynolds (top)

William Blake — a bronze bust by Sir Jacob Epstein (bottom)

George III and the Royal Family. It was at a similar performance in 1791 that the king rose to his feet during the singing of the "Hallelujah Chorus" and established a custom which is now observed wherever *Messiah* is performed.

Most of the other famous musicians are buried or have memorials in the north choir aisle where the great Henry Purcell is buried and where the organ used to stand until 1730. Among them are Orlando Gibbons, John Blow, William Croft and other organists of the Abbey in the seventeenth and eighteenth centuries, while 20th century music is represented by Edward Elgar, Ralph Vaughan Williams and, most recently, Benjamin Britten. Muzio Clementi who died in 1832 and is sometimes called "the father of the pianoforte" is buried in the south walk of the Great Cloister.

The London theatre of the eighteenth century produced many notable actors and actresses, a number of whom were popular enough to warrant national recognition with burial or memorialisation in the Abbey or its precincts. Ann Olfdield (1683-1730) who was considered to be the greatest actress of her day, was buried in the nave after a splendid funeral, and her contemporary, Barton Booth, was given a monument in Poets' Corner. The Chapel of St. Andrew has statues of the actor John Kemple (1757-1823) and of his sister, Sarah Siddons, a famous actress. Thomas Betterton (1635-1710), who spent 50 years on the stage, is buried in the east walk of the Great Cloister, and near him is Anne Bracegirdle, who was brought up in his household and became a very popular actress.

Pride of place in this galaxy of stage stars has been given to the greatest of them all, David Garrick, who retired at the height of his fame in 1776, and whose funeral procession three years later is said to have extended from the Adelphi, where he lived, to the Abbey where he was buried. His statue in Poets' Corner portrays him on the stage, taking his final curtain-call. Not far away, in the south choir aisle, is the grave of Dame Sybil Thorndike, who died in 1976, aged 94,

KEATS
1795-1821

SHELLEY
1792-1822

1759 BURNS 1796

ROBERT SOUTHEY.
BORN AUGUST 12T 1774, DIED MARCH 21T 1843.

GVLIELMO·SHAKSPEARE
ANNO·POST·MORTEM·CXXIV
AMOR·PVBLICVS·POSVIT

JOHNSON

JANE
AUSTEN
1775
1817

WILLIAM SHAKESPEARE 1564~1616
BURIED AT STRATFORD-ON-AVON

JAMES THOMSON

CHARLOTTE BRONTE
1816 1855
EMILY JANE BRONTE
1818 1848
ANNE BRONTE
1820 1849

WILLIAM WORDSWORTH

A festal altar frontal and hanging designed for the
Coronation of King George V

and was one of the finest actresses of her time as well as a frequent worshipper in Westminster Abbey. Her gravestone has a moving verse epitaph based on some lines written in honour of her 80th birthday by J.B. Priestley.

TREASURES — OLD AND NEW

Anyone unacquainted with the course of English history could be forgiven for supposing that a church as ancient and royal as Westminster Abbey possessed a great hoard of artistic treasures. So it once did. In 1388 there were 307 copes, 34 candlesticks, 9 crosses and 13 chalices, besides statues, paintings and rich hangings.

But when the monastery was dissolved in 1540 most of these treasures were seized by King Henry VIII and within a few years the building was bare. During the early part of the seventeenth century the Abbey was re-equipped on the lavish scale that seemed appropriate to a royal church, but by the middle of the same century the Puritans had stripped the place bare again.

On the restoration of the monarchy in 1660, the Dean and Chapter had virtually to start afresh and during the course of the next two years they purchased some superb silver-gilt plate — chalices and patens, flagons for the wine at the Holy Communion, and alms dishes. At the same time copes were made in deep red and dark purple velvet, decorated with pomegranates and stars of silver and gold. Tradition asserts that these copes were actually used at the Coronation of King Charles II, and they are worn quite frequently at the Abbey's services today, being in excellent condition.

More Communion plate was added later in the seventeenth century and in 1691 the Abbey received one of its most splendid, and certainly one of its most touching, gifts. Sarah Hughes had for many years been the maid or housekeeper of Dr. Thomas Knipe, a distinguished under-master, and later Headmaster, of Westminster School. She was a regular worshipper in the Abbey and on her death left sufficient money, £ 80, from her life savings for the purchase of the magnificent pair of candlesticks that have stood on the high altar ever since. These are of silver-gilt, exquisitely decorated with bands of cherubs and festoons of flowers.

Little was added to the Abbey's treasures during the eighteenth and nineteenth centuries, but the Coronation of King Edward VII in 1902 saw the acquisition of some fine fabrics. At every Coronation the Sovereign makes an offering of an ingot of gold and an altar cloth. In the present century this symbolic offering has sometimes been enlarged to include a set of

An altar candlestick   *A festal cope, woven in France*

Processional banner (top left)

The main processional cross (top right)

Rose window in the transept (bottom left)

copes, and those provided by King Edward VII are of richly embroidered red velvet.

The main processional cross was the gift of an American, the Hon. Rodman Wanamaker, in 1922. This is made of silver-gilt and ivory and has a number of plaques of gold engraved with scenes from the life of Christ and other religious themes. The cross is also studded with sapphires and for the 900th anniversary

Coronation portrait of King Richard II in the Nave

of the Abbey's foundation a descendant of the donor added 72 diamonds.

The present century has seen the steady acquisition of beautiful objects for the enrichment of the Abbey's worship. At their wedding in 1922, the then Duke and Duchess of York, later to become King George VI and Queen Elizabeth, presented a pair of silver candlesticks for the altar in the Chapel of St. Edward. Queen Elizabeth II gave an interesting set of blue copes, adorned with heraldic beasts, at the Coronation in 1953, and more recently a generous bequest has enabled the Abbey to obtain a set of white and gold copes, woven in Lyons on the same looms that were used for the furnishings of Versailles in the time of Louis XVI.

Very little of the Abbey's mediaeval glass remains and the six medallions of thirteenth century glass incorporated into the north window of the Jerusalem Chamber indicate how much of beauty was lost at the Reformation. Apart from these medallions, there are some fragments of old glass in the east window, high in the apse, including a portrayal of St. Edward holding out a ring to St. John the Evangelist, dating from about 1490. In a small window at the west end of the nave, in the Warriors' Chapel, some mediaeval fragments have been pieced together to make a new design.

The Rose window in the north transept and the Great West window are fine examples of early eighteenth century painted glass, and on the north side of the nave there is a series of early twentieth century windows portraying various kings and abbots associated with the building of the nave.

Tower of St. Margaret's Church

Interior of St. Margaret's Church

THE CHURCH OF ST. MARGARET

Standing in the shadow of Westminster Abbey, and dwarfed by its vast size, is St. Margaret's Church — until recently the oldest parish church in Westminster and now incorporated into the jurisdiction of the Dean and Chapter. St. Margaret's is in fact a very large church with a long and interesting history of its own.

Mediaeval abbeys and cathedrals were not designed for regular use by ordinary people. In the case of Westminster Abbey, it was primarily the church of a community of monks, with their own disciplined life and patterns of worship, and a place where kings and queen were crowned and buried. A multitude of pilgrims visited the shrine of St. Edward the Confessor and the Abbey was often crowded, but it did not, and could not, provide a spiritual home for the people who lived in the neighbourhood. Hence the building of a parish church to meet local needs.

According to one tradition, St. Margaret's was — like the Abbey itself — founded by King Edward the Confessor, but the evidence for this is not conclusive. The earliest mention of the church is in a document dating from the first half of the twelfth century. At the time the parish was very large, covering the greater part of what is now London's busy West End, though the population was small and scattered. A document issued on behalf of the Pope in 1222 confirmed that St. Margaret's was under the jurisdiction of the Ab-

Statue of Oliver Cromwell who worshipped in St. Margaret's (top)

The East Window (bottom)

bot of Westminster and not under the Bishop of London.

The present church dates from 1523 and was being built — probably as a replacement for a Norman building — at the same time as the Chapel of King Henry VII next door. Seventeen years later the monastery was dissolved and King Henry's henchmen not only pillaged the Abbey but also laid violent hands on the beautiful furnishings of St. Margaret's. At one moment it seemed that the church itself might be demolished to provide building materials for a new palace being built on the banks of the Thames for the Duke of Somerset but the parishioners, armed with bows and clubs and staves, drove off the workmen when they attempted to start the demolition, so the church was spared. The exterior was heavily restored in 1735, when the tower was rebuilt.

One of the chief glories of St. Margaret's is its east window which houses some of the finest painted glass in England. It was made in Flanders sometime between 1515 and may have been a wedding gift to King Henry VIII and Princess Catherine of Aragon, whose portraits are in the bottom right and left corners. There is some, not quite conclusive, evidence that it was originally installed in Waltham Abbey, but by 1758 the window was in private hands and in that year the House of Commons bought it and presented it to St. Margaret's. Two other large windows, in the west wall of the church, were presented by American friends in 1888 — one commemorates Sir Walter Raleigh, the other John Milton. The windows on the south side are the work of John Piper and replaced glass destroyed during World War II.

The close association of the House of Commons with St. Margaret's goes back to 1614 when, on Palm Sunday, the whole House gathered in the church to receive the Holy Communion. Similar corporate Communions were held on three other occasions but after the restoration of the monarchy in 1660 they were replaced by regular sermons preached before the Speaker of the House of Commons and Members of Parliament. These continued until 1859.

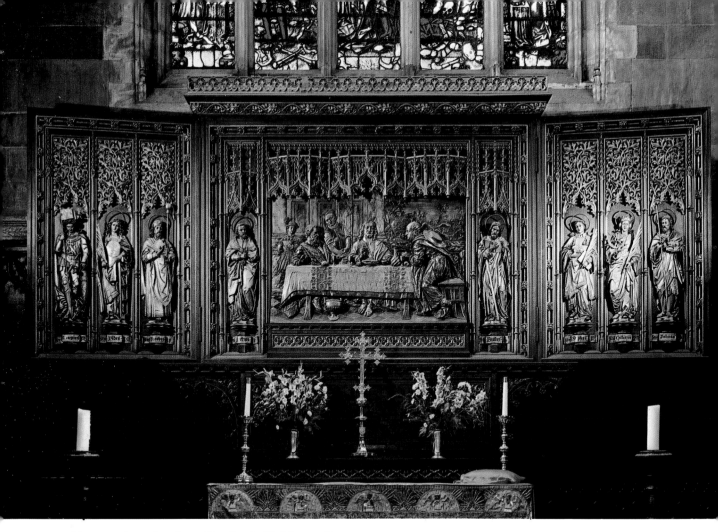

Lime wood reredos above the altar in St. Margaret's

Since then it has been customary for the House of Commons to repair to St. Margaret's to give thanks to God for a great national deliverance, as for example the ending of the Crimean War (1856), the First World War (1918) and the Second World War (1945). The Speaker still has his own seat in the church and the Canon of the Abbey who is the Rector of St. Margaret's is usually invited to serve as Speaker's Chaplain. This involves him in conducting prayers in the House of Commons every day when Parliament is sitting.

Many famous people have been associated with St. Margaret's over the years. Geoffrey Chaucer, the great mediaeval poet, was a regular worshipper in the late fourteenth century, and a hundred years later his *Canterbury Tales* were first printed by another member of the congregation, William Caxton, who had opened his pioneering printing shop close by. On 20 October 1618 Sir Walter Raleigh, Elizabethan poet and writer and the coloniser of Virginia, was beheaded on a scaffold erected just outside St. Margaret's and his body was buried under the high altar of the church.

Later in the same century, one of England's greatest poets, John Milton, was often to be seen in St. Margaret's, as also was Samuel Pepys, the diarist, who recorded his pleasure at the sight of so many beautiful women in the congregation. In the present century Sir Winston Churchill, destined to become one of Britain's greatest Prime Ministers, was married in St. Margaret's in 1908. Today the church is more closely integrated with Westminster Abbey than at any time in its history, and seeks to minister to the large number of people who spend their working life in Westminster — in the service of government and commerce.

Contents

ACKNOWLEDGEMENTS

The author and publisher gratefully acknowledge the generous co-operation of the Dean and Chapter of Westminster Abbey in the preparation of this book. The photographs were taken specially by the staff photographer of FISA Industrias Gráficas with the exception of the following which appear by arrangement with the copyright holders: Dean and Chapter of Westminster Abbey, Arms of Westminster Abbey on the title page and front cover and the plan facing the title page; Aerofilms Ltd., page 2; Mary Evans Picture Library, page 4 (bottom); the Syndics of Cambridge University, page 5 (top); the Governors of Dulwich Picture Gallery, 54 (top); National Portrait Gallery 31 and 46; Fox Photos Ltd., 25 and back cover; Crown Copyright reserved and reproduced with permission of the Controller of Her Majesty's Stationery Office, 43 (bottom) and 7; Camera Press Ltd., 16; The Press Association Ltd., 15; Woodmansterne Publications Ltd., front cover (Clive Friend) and 40 (Drake Brookshaw, after a drawing by A.E. Henderson); Trustees of the British Museum, 41 (bottom left). Picture research by Eric Restall.

Collection ALL EUROPE

#		Spanish	French	English	German	Italian	Catalan	Dutch	Swedish	Portuguese	Japanese	Finnish
1	ANDORRA	●	●	●	●	●	●					
2	LISBON	●	●	●	●	●				●		
3	LONDON	●	●	●	●	●					●	
4	BRUGES	●	●	●	●	●		●				
5	PARIS	●	●	●	●	●					●	
6	MONACO	●	●	●	●	●						
7	VIENNA	●	●	●	●	●						
11	VERDUN	●	●	●	●					●		
12	THE TOWER OF LONDON	●	●	●	●							
13	ANTWERP	●	●	●	●	●		●				
14	WESTMINSTER ABBEY	●	●	●	●							
15	THE SPANISH RIDING SCHOOL IN VIENNA	●	●	●	●							
16	FATIMA	●	●	●	●	●				●		
17	WINDSOR CASTLE	●	●	●	●	●					●	
19	COTE D'AZUR	●	●	●	●	●						
22	BRUSSELS	●	●	●	●	●		●				
23	SCHÖNBRUNN PALACE	●	●	●	●	●		●				
24	ROUTE OF PORT WINE	●	●	●	●	●				●		
26	HOFBURG PALACE	●	●	●	●	●						
27	ALSACE	●	●	●	●	●		●				
31	MALTA			●	●	●						
32	PERPIGNAN		●									
33	STRASBOURG											
34	MADEIRA + PORTO SANTO	●	●	●						●		
35	CERDAGNE - CAPCIR		●				●					
36	BERLIN	●	●	●	●	●						

Collection ART IN SPAIN

#		Spanish	French	English	German	Italian	Catalan	Dutch	Swedish	Portuguese	Japanese	Finnish
1	PALAU DE LA MUSICA CATALANA	●		●		●						
2	GAUDI	●	●	●	●	●					●	
3	PRADO MUSEUM I (Spanish Painting)	●	●	●	●	●					●	
4	PRADO MUSEUM II (Foreign Painting)	●	●	●	●	●						
5	MONASTERY OF GUADALUPE	●										
6	THE CASTLE OF XAVIER	●	●	●	●						●	
7	THE FINE ARTS MUSEUM OF SEVILLE	●	●	●	●							
8	SPANISH CASTLES	●	●	●								
9	THE CATHEDRALS OF SPAIN	●	●	●								
10	THE CATHEDRAL OF GERONA	●	●	●								
14	PICASSO	●	●	●	●						●	
15	REALES ALCAZARES (ROYAL PALACE OF SEVILLE)	●	●	●	●							
16	MADRID'S ROYAL PALACE	●	●	●	●							
17	ROYAL MONASTERY OF EL ESCORIAL	●	●	●	●							
18	THE WINES OF CATALONIA	●										
19	THE ALHAMBRA AND THE GENERALIFE	●										
20	GRANADA AND THE ALHAMBRA	●										
21	ROYAL ESTATE OF ARANJUEZ	●	●	●	●	●						
22	ROYAL ESTATE OF EL PARDO	●	●	●	●	●						
23	ROYAL HOUSES	●	●	●	●							
24	ROYAL PALACE OF SAN ILDEFONSO	●	●	●	●	●						
25	HOLY CROSS OF THE VALLE DE LOS CAIDOS	●	●	●	●							
26	OUR LADY OF THE PILLAR OF SARAGOSSA	●	●	●	●							
27	TEMPLE DE LA SAGRADA FAMILIA	●	●	●	●	●	●					
28	POBLET ABTEI	●	●	●	●			●				

Collection ALL SPAIN

#		Spanish	French	English	German	Italian	Catalan	Dutch	Swedish	Portuguese	Japanese	Finnish
1	ALL MADRID	●	●	●	●	●					●	
2	ALL BARCELONA	●	●	●	●	●	●					
3	ALL SEVILLE	●	●	●	●	●					●	
4	ALL MAJORCA	●	●	●	●	●						
5	ALL THE COSTA BRAVA	●	●	●	●	●						
6	ALL MALAGA and the Costa del Sol	●	●	●	●	●			●			
7	ALL THE CANARY ISLANDS (Gran Canaria)	●	●	●	●	●			●	●		
8	ALL CORDOBA	●	●	●	●	●					●	
9	ALL GRANADA	●	●	●	●	●		●			●	
10	ALL VALENCIA	●	●	●	●	●						
11	ALL TOLEDO	●	●	●	●	●						
12	ALL SANTIAGO	●	●	●	●							
13	ALL IBIZA and Formentera	●	●	●	●	●						
14	ALL CADIZ and the Costa de la Luz	●	●	●	●							
15	ALL MONTSERRAT	●	●	●	●	●		●				
16	ALL SANTANDER and Cantabria	●										
17	ALL THE CANARY ISLANDS II, (Tenerife)	●	●	●	●	●						●
20	ALL BURGOS	●	●	●	●							
21	ALL ALICANTE and the Costa Blanca	●	●	●	●	●						
22	ALL NAVARRA	●	●	●	●							
23	ALL LERIDA	●	●	●	●			●				
24	ALL SEGOVIA	●	●	●	●							
25	ALL SARAGOSSA	●	●	●	●							
26	ALL SALAMANCA	●	●	●	●						●	
27	ALL AVILA	●	●	●	●							
28	ALL MINORCA	●	●	●	●	●						
29	ALL SAN SEBASTIAN and Guipúzcoa	●										
30	ALL ASTURIAS	●		●								
31	ALL LA CORUNNA and the Rías Altas	●	●	●								
32	ALL TARRAGONA	●	●	●		●						
33	ALL MURCIA	●	●	●								
34	ALL VALLADOLID	●	●	●								
35	ALL GIRONA	●	●	●								
36	ALL HUESCA	●	●									
37	ALL JAEN	●	●	●								
38	ALL ALMERIA	●	●	●								
40	ALL CUENCA	●	●	●								
41	ALL LEON	●	●	●								
42	ALL PONTEVEDRA, VIGO and the Rías Bajas	●	●	●								
43	ALL RONDA	●	●	●	●	●		●				
44	ALL SORIA	●										
46	ALL EXTREMADURA	●										
47	ALL ANDALUSIA	●	●	●	●	●						
52	ALL MORELLA	●	●				●					

Collection ALL AMERICA

#		Spanish	French	English	German	Italian	Catalan	Dutch	Swedish	Portuguese	Japanese	Finnish
1	PUERTO RICO	●		●								
2	SANTO DOMINGO	●		●								
3	QUEBEC			●	●							
4	COSTA RICA	●										
5	CARACAS	●		●								

Collection ALL AFRICA

#		Spanish	French	English	German	Italian	Catalan	Dutch	Swedish	Portuguese	Japanese	Finnish
1	MOROCCO	●	●	●	●	●						
2	THE SOUTH OF MOROCCO	●	●	●	●	●						
3	TUNISIA			●	●	●						
4	RWANDA		●									

The printing of this book was completed
in the workshops of
FISA - ESCUDO DE ORO, S.A.